David was sick with a cold. He had been out of school for three days. Now he was getting better, and he was also getting bored!

David could read and draw while he was sick. But it was hard to stay home all day with no one to talk to. His mother was there, but she had work to do.

David lay there in the stillness.
"It's so quiet here," he thought. David closed
his eyes. Then he heard a funny sound.

"Caw! Caw! Caw!"

David opened his eyes. "What was that?" he said.

The sound went on.

"Caw! Caw! Caw!"

David could tell that the sound wasn't from anything in the house. He quickly looked out. There were big black birds all over the ground!

"They must be crows," thought David.
"One, two, three . . . seven, eight, nine . . ."
More crows were flying in. David finally gave up
trying to tell how many crows there were.

David's mother came in.

"Mom, look at all the crows out there!" said David.

Mother looked out. "My goodness!" she said. "I never saw so many crows in one place before."

The crows were eating something on the ground.
Still more crows flew in.

"What do you think they found out there?"
asked David. "It must be something good."

"They could have found some seeds they like," said Mom. "But crows will eat nearly anything."

"Where did they all come from?" David asked.

"I think they have left a cold place, to fly to one that's warmer," said Mom. "They're just stopping here for a little while in between, to get something to eat."

In the light from the sun, the crows looked blue-black and shiny.

"They're kind of pretty," said David.

"I think so too, but they're not at all pretty to the farmers!" Mom said. "Farmers don't like crows very much. Crows are harmful because they eat the crops. Farmers are always trying to make crows go away."

All at once, the cat from next door came by.
She started to stalk one of the crows by sneaking
up in back of it.

The crow turned around. It was nearly as big as the cat, and it wasn't afraid at all.

"Caw! Caw! Caw!" went the crow.

The cat turned and ran away as fast as it could! David and his mother had a good laugh!

They watched the crows for about one hour. Then, with a few more "Caw-caws," the crows finally flew away.

"I liked seeing the crows," said David. "I want them to come back next year. Then I'll have to get sick again, so I can stay home and watch them!"

"We'll have to see about that," said Mom.

By the next day, David was all better, so he went back to school.

"Did you get bored staying home for so many days?" his friend Jake asked.

"No," said David. "I had a great time watching some crows."

Jake gave David a funny look. "CROWS?"
said Jake. "You MUST have been sick!"
Jake was laughing, but David didn't care,
because Jake didn't know what he had missed.